KIDDYWINK CREW
ACTIVITIES FOR YOU!
SERIES 1
ANIMALS, ALPHABET, NUMBERS

SCAN THE QR CODE TO LISTEN TO THE PODCAST!

WRITTEN & DESIGNED BY: JULIANNA BRIA & LINDSAY FARLEY
FOUNDERS OF KIDDYWINK CREW
COLORING PAGES CREATED BY: ALEX PALMA

DEDICATED TO OUR VERY OWN KIDDYWINKS

KIDDYWINK
CREW

ACTIVITIES FOR YOU!
SERIES 1
ANIMALS, ALPHABET, NUMBERS

Kiddywink Crew LLC

ISBN: 979-8-9890218-0-2

TABLE OF CONTENTS

Thank you for supporting our business!
We hope you have a BLAST working on this book!

Aa

YOUR TURN!

Your turn! At the end of each Kiddywink Crew episode, we give ideas of what to draw. Listen for our idea, or get creative and draw your own picture here!

Directions: Ari and his buddies keep losing teeth! Help them figure out how many teeth they have left by **subtracting**/shading in the "teeth tens frame", and filling in the equations.

EXAMPLE:

Ari had 10 teeth. Then he lost 1. How many does he have left?

 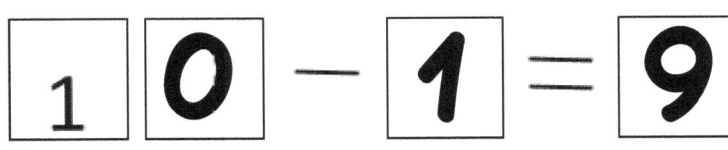

Ari has 9 teeth left.

Alex had 10 teeth. Then she lost 3. How many does she have left?

 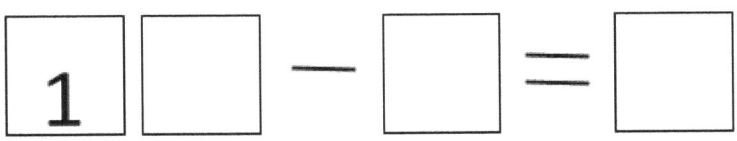

Alex has _____ teeth left.

Ali had 10 teeth. Then she lost 6. How many does she have left?

 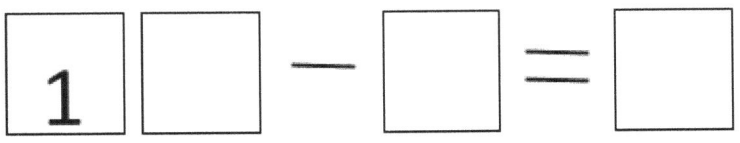

Ali has _____ teeth left.

Alan had 10 teeth. Then he lost 5. How many does he have left?

 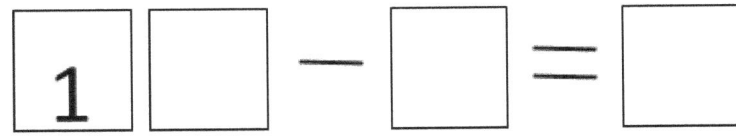

Alan has _____ teeth left.

KIDDYWINK

Aa

Alligator

YOUR TURN!

You know what to do, Kiddywink Crew!
Draw your picture here!

BABOON BUDDIES

Directions: Bailey and Bruce love being together, and because there are 2 of them, they make a perfect pair! With **even** numbers, everyone has a partner. With **odd** numbers, someone is left out. Are these numbers odd or even?

EXAMPLE:

There were 5 baboons. Did everyone have a partner? Is 5 odd or even?

5 is ODD – one baboon was left out.

There were 8 baboons. Did everyone have a partner? Is 8 odd or even?

There were 6 baboons. Did everyone have a partner? Is 6 odd or even?

There were 9 baboons. Did everyone have a partner? Is 9 odd or even?

There were 10 baboons. Did everyone have a partner? Is 10 odd or even?

There were 7 baboons. Did everyone have a partner? Is 7 odd or even?

KIDDYWINK

Bb

Baboon

You know what to do, Kiddywink Crew!
Draw your picture here!

 CAMEL SNOW CONES

Directions: **Skip count** _by 2 and 3! Carmen and her friends love to try different flavors of snow cones. Count along on their adventure and see how many flavors they try._

EXAMPLE:
There were 3 flavors of snow cones to choose from. Carmen got 3 of each flavor to share with her friends. How many snow cones did she get in all?

There were 9 snow cones in all.

There were 4 flavors of snow cones to choose from. Carmen got 2 orders of each flavor to share with her friends. How many snow cones did she get in all?

There were 5 flavors of snow cones to choose from. Carmen got 2 orders of each flavor to share with her friends. How many snow cones did she get in all?

There were 2 flavors of snow cones to choose from. Carmen got 3 orders of each flavor to share with her friends. How many snow cones did she get in all?

There were 4 flavors of snow cones to choose from. Carmen got 3 orders of each flavor to share with her friends. How many snow cones did she get in all?

Challenge:
There were 6 snow cone flavors to choose from. Carmen got 3 orders each of 3 flavors and 2 orders each of the other 3 flavors. How many did she get in all?

Cc

Camel

Dd

YOUR TURN!

You know what to do, Kiddywink Crew!
Draw your picture here!

DUCKLINGS AND THE FOUR SEASONS

Directions: *Mrs. Quackie, Dylan's teacher, asked her students to pick their favorite season. Dylan picked fall because that's when her family leaves for Florida each year. Help Mrs. Quackie and her students* **analyze the data**.

Here is the **data** she collected:

Summer	‖‖‖ ‖‖
Fall	‖‖
Winter	‖‖‖
Spring	‖‖‖ ‖

How many ducklings chose summer as their favorite season? _____

Which season had the fewest votes? _____

How many ducklings answered the question? _____

Complete the bar graph below by shading in the correct amount of spaces for each season:

Dd

Duckling

Ee

YOUR TURN!

You know what to do, Kiddywink Crew!
Draw your picture here!

ELENA COMPARES HEIGHTS

Directions: _Elena the emu is 5 feet tall._ **Compare** _her height to other animals._

EXAMPLE::

Bailey the baboon is 2 feet tall. Who is taller? By how many feet?

Elena is 3 feet taller than Bailey
5 – 2 = 3
2 + 3 = 5

Carmen the camel is 6 feet tall. Who is taller? By how much?

Ghulam the giraffe is 16 feet tall. Who is taller? By how much?

Hidi the hippo is 4 feet tall. Who is taller? By how much?

Victoria the velociraptor is 7 feet tall. Who is taller? By how much?

Challenge: Dylan the duckling is 4 _inches_ tall. Who is taller? By how much?

Ee

Emu

Ff

Frank Flies Fast

25

You know what to do, Kiddywink Crew!
Draw your picture here!

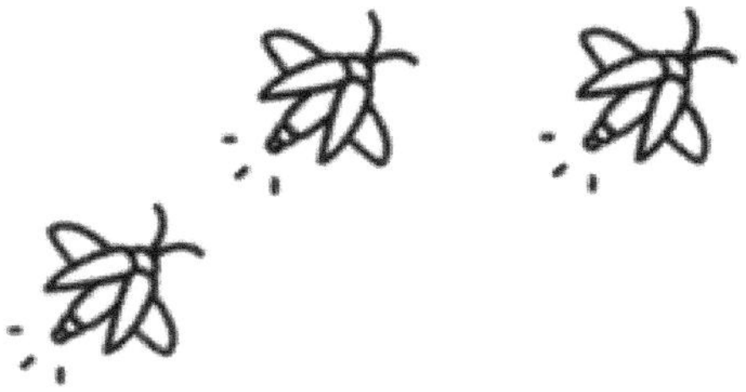

RACING FIREFLIES

Can you help Frank and his buddies race to the finish line?!

Materials: 3 Playing Pieces (egos, cheerios, paperclips, etc.) and 1 Regular Die.

Players: 1 - 3 Players

Directions:
1. Place the 3 playing pieces on the 3 start spots.
2. Roll 1 die.
3. Decide which "firefly" or "fireflies" you would like to move. For example, if you roll a 6 you could move one firefly 2 spaces and the other firefly 4 spaces - that is called decomposing the number! Or you could move one firefly 6 spaces.
4. Work together with your partner, taking turns, to get all the fireflies to the finish line.
5. You do not need an exact amount to get to the finish line, you just need to reach the finish line to complete the game.

Challenge: Add another die, and work on adding the dice and then decomposing the number.

10! Finish Line!

START

START

START

Ff

Firefly

Gg

You know what to do, Kiddywink Crew!
Draw your picture here!

GHULAM'S SPOTTY SPOTS

Directions: _Ghulam was born with 7 spots. He's perfect just the way he is, but for fun, can you help him_ **add more**_?_

EXAMPLE:

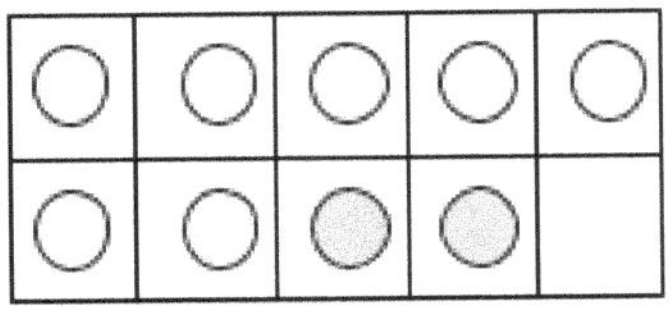

Ghulam had 7 spots. After he added some he had 9. How many did he add?

$$7 \quad + \quad 2 \quad = \quad 9$$

Ghulam added **2** spcts.

Use the 20 frame to help

Ghulam had 7 spots. After he added some he had 17. How many did he add?

$$\square \quad + \quad \square\square \quad = \quad \square\square$$

Ghulam added _____ spots.

Use the 20 frame to help

Ghulam had 7 spots. After he added some he had 13. How many did he add?

$$\square \quad + \quad \square \quad = \quad \square\square$$

Ghulam added _____ spots.

Use the 20 frame to help

Ghulam had 7 spots. After he added some he had 11. How many did he add?

$$\square \quad + \quad \square \quad = \quad \square\square$$

Ghulam added _____ spots.

31

Gg

Giraffe

Hh

You know what to do, Kiddywink Crew!
Draw your picture here!

HIPPOS HOLDING THEIR BREATH

*Directions: Hidi still needs to work on holding her breath. Help her fill out these clocks, and calculate **elapsed time** (the time that has passed), for swim practice.*

EXAMPLE:

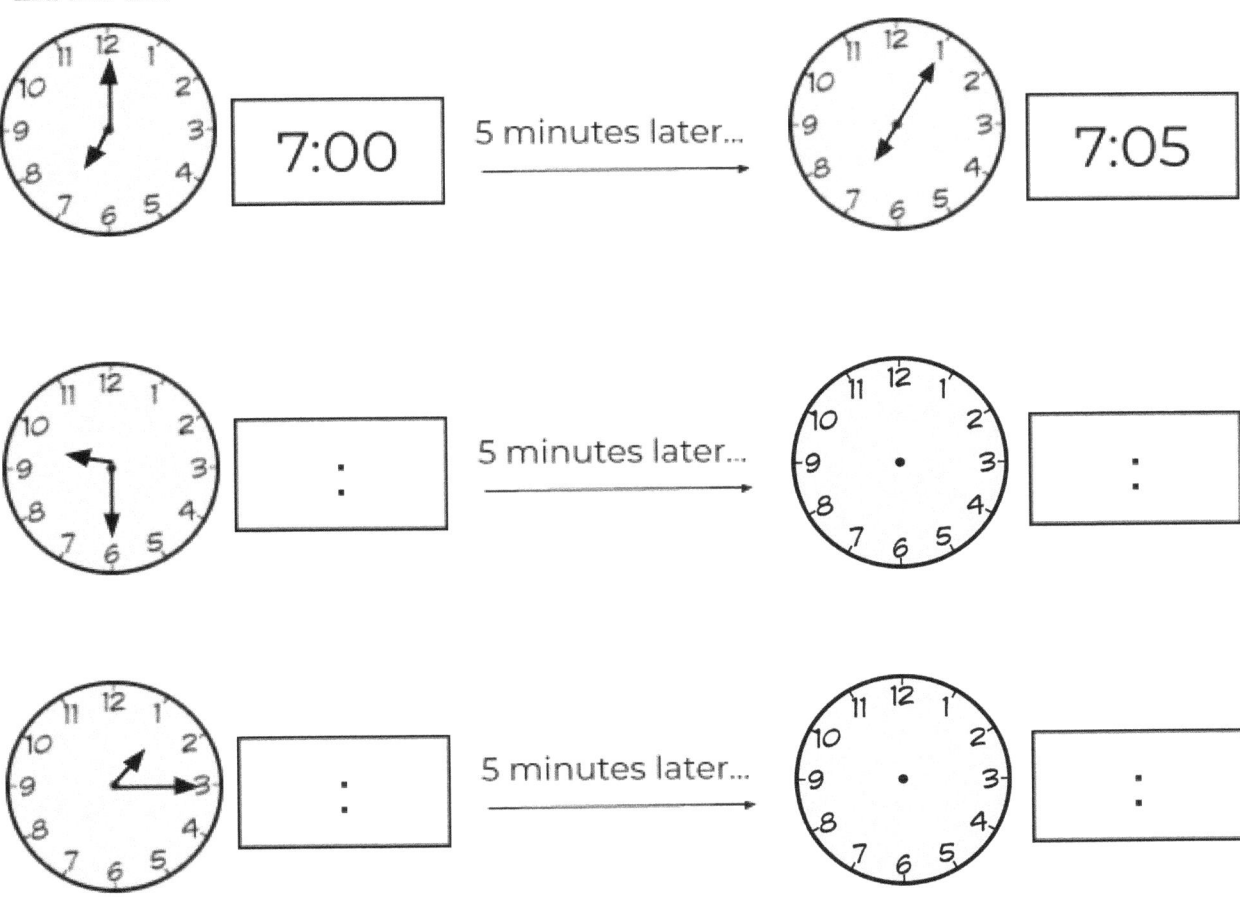

Elapsed Time without Clocks
Hidi was practicing holding her breath. She started at 6:20 pm. She held her breath for 5 minutes. What time was it when she finished?

Challenge:
Hidi was practicing holding her breath. She started at 11:58 am. She held her breath for 5 minutes. What time was it when she finished?

Hh

Hippo

YOUR TURN!

You know what to do, Kiddywink Crew!
Draw your picture here!

Directions: _There is a lot of_ **mixed up math** _in Mrs. Iman's class! Have fun solving it with Izzy and Iliad!_

Time

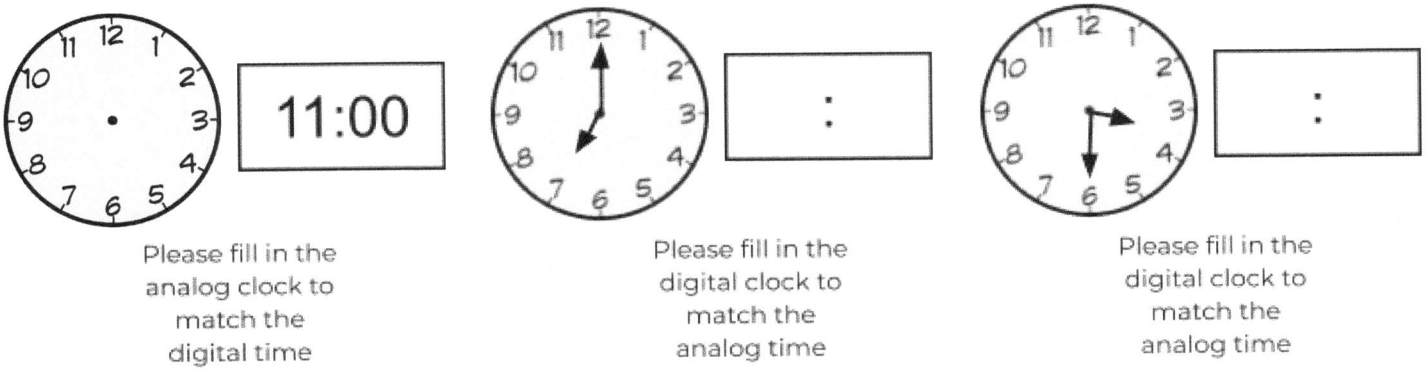

Please fill in the analog clock to match the digital time

Please fill in the digital clock to match the analog time

Please fill in the digital clock to match the analog time

Mixed Operations

There are typically 18 students in Mrs. Iman's class. The other day, 2 boys and 3 girls were out sick. How many kids were at school that day?

Mrs. Iman left 12 lettuce pieces out for Iliad and Izzy. After they ate some, there were 8 pieces of lettuce left. How many pieces of lettuce did they eat?

Geometry

There are 18 students in Mrs. Iman's class. There is one rectangular table, one square table, and one circle table. How many people do you think are at each table? Please draw a picture to show where everyone could sit. *Hint: there are many answers to this one. Feel free to use an extra blank page to show multiple options!

KIDDYWINK

Ii

Iguana

YOUR TURN!

You know what to do, Kiddywink Crew!
Draw your picture here!

JEROME COUNTS BACKWARDS

Directions: *Jerome likes to count backwards to calm down. Can you fill in the missing numbers in his **backwards patterns**? Sometimes he likes to count backwards by 1s, and sometimes by 10s.*

Counting Backwards by 1s

EXAMPLE:

10	9	8	7	6	5	4	3	2	1	0

21	20		18	17	16				12	

33			30			27	26	25		

Counting Backwards by 10s

100	90	80				40	30	20		0

92	82			52	42		

113		93	83			53	

CHALLENGE: Counting Backwards by?

		20		14					

36			27		21			12		

KIDDYWINK

Jj

Jellyfish

 **YOUR TURN!**

You know what to do, Kiddywink Crew!
Draw your picture here!

KAYLA'S SHARE-AND-TELL PARTY BALLOONS

*Directions: Kayla was finding some balloons for a share-and-tell party. She wants all the balloons that equal 11. Can you POP (cross out) the balloons that **don't equal 11**?*

EXAMPLE:

10 + 2

10 + 1   7 + 2   20 - 9   9 + 4

10 - 2   5 + 7   5 + 2 + 5   3 + 8

7 + 5   12 - 1   6 + 5   11 + 1   3 + 7

11 - 0   6 + 1 + 4   13 - 2   8 + 4

47

KIDDYWINK

Kk

Koala

LI

You know what to do, Kiddywink Crew!
Draw your picture here!

Directions: Louise and Larry love that they add up to 12. They also love that their kids add up to 12! Can you make each of these ladybug pairs **add up to 12** spots too?

EXAMPLE:

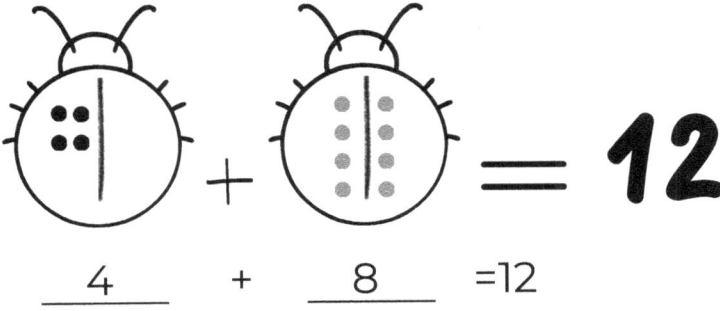

4 + 8 =12

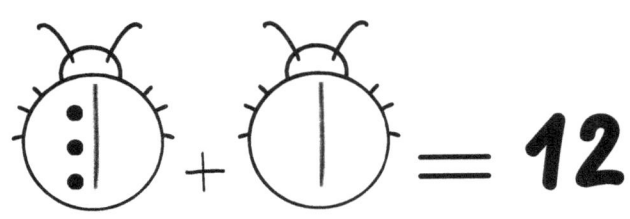

_____ + _____ =12

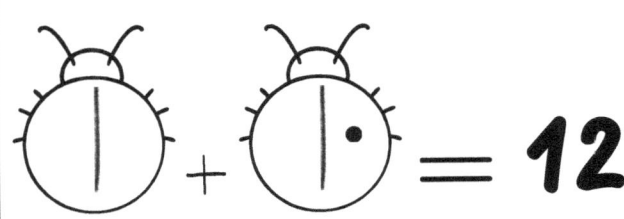

_____ + _____ =12

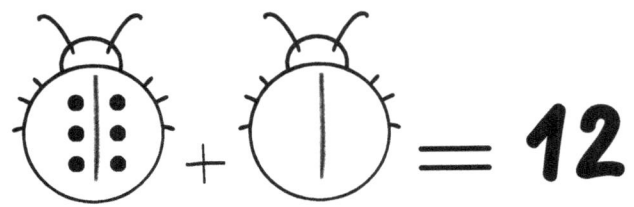

_____ + _____ =12

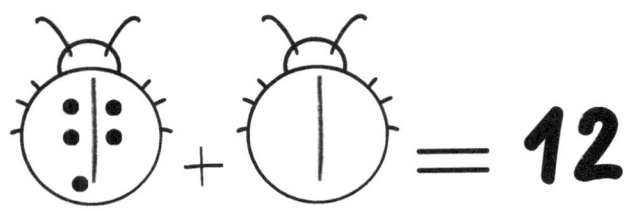

_____ + _____ =12

_____ + _____ =12

_____ + _____ =12

Ll

Ladybug

Mm

You know what to do, Kiddywink Crew!
Draw your picture here!

DETECTIVE MOHAMMED HELPS MOLES SHARE FAIRLY

Directions: *Sharing can be tricky, especially when it's an odd amount, but it can be done!* **Split** *these earthworms* **fairly** *- Mohammed, and YOU, know how to do it!*

EXAMPLE:

Mohammed and Michael had 11 earthworms. They wanted to split them equally. How many did they each get?

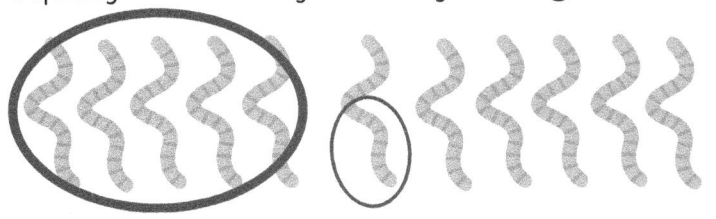

They each got 5 and a half (or 5 ½) earthworms

Mohammed and Michael had 9 earthworms. They wanted to split them equally. How many did they each get?

Mohammed and Michael had 12 earthworms. They wanted to split them equally. How many did they each get?

Mohammed and Michael had 15 earthworms. They wanted to split them equally. How many did they each get?

Challenges:

Mohammed, Michael, and <u>you</u> had 12 earthworms. You all wanted to split them equally. How many did each of you get?

Mohammed, Michael, <u>you</u>, and your friend had 19 earthworms. You all wanted to split them equally. How many did each of you get?

KIDDYWINK CREW

Mm

Mole

You know what to do, Kiddywink Crew!
Draw your picture here!

THE NOTE FAMILY SCHEDULES THEIR PERFORMANCE

Directions: Lucky 14 Jazz Club needs help **scheduling** their next performers. They book 2 weeks from when a singer calls. Can you help them?

EXAMPLE:

The Note family called on March 2nd to book a show. When are they scheduled to sing?

March

2	3	4	5	6	7	8
9	10	11	12	13	14	15
⑯						

1 week
2 weeks

2 + 14 (days in 2 weeks) = **16**
They will perform there on March 16th!

The Songbirds called on April 11th to book a show. When are they scheduled?

The Parrots called on June 5th to book a show. When are they scheduled?

The Pigeons also called on June 5th to book a show. The Parrots were already scheduled for 2 weeks from then, so they scheduled the Pigeons for 3 weeks from the 5th. When do they come in for their show?

Challenges:

The Woodpeckers called on February 20th to book a show. It is not a leap year so there are 28 days in February. When are they scheduled?

The Parakeets called on July 29th (There are 31 days in July) to book a show. When are they scheduled?

KIDDYWINK

Nn

Nightingale

YOUR TURN!

You know what to do, Kiddywink Crew!
Draw your picture here!

HELP OZZIE DECORATE

Directions: Ozzie bought lots of supplies for Sammy the Seahorse's birthday party! And with his 8 arms, he can set up for the party quickly. It's your job to figure out the **number of party supplies** he's holding at once. Don't forget that Ozzie has 8 arms (two are hidden behind him).

EXAMPLE:
Ozzie was holding two double bubble brownie bars in each tentacle. How many bars was he holding?

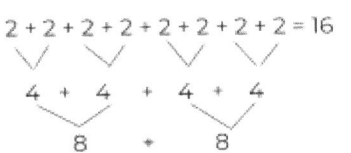   OR $2 \times 8 = 16$

He was holding 16 double bubble brownie bars.

Ozzie was holding rolls of streamers. He was holding 4 rolls in each tentacle. How many rolls did he have?

Ozzie was carrying balloons. He had 6 balloons in each tentacle. How many balloons did he have?

Ozzie was holding Sammy's presents for him. He had 3 presents in each tentacle. How many presents did he have?

Ozzie loves pool floaties and got a bunch for the party. He had 7 floaties in each tentacle. How many pool floaties did he have?

Challenge:
Everyone got their very own puzzle as a party favor! Ozzie loves puzzles and did his right away. The puzzle had 40 pieces. He wanted to hold an equal number of puzzle pieces in each tentacle. How many puzzle pieces should he have had in each tentacle?

Oo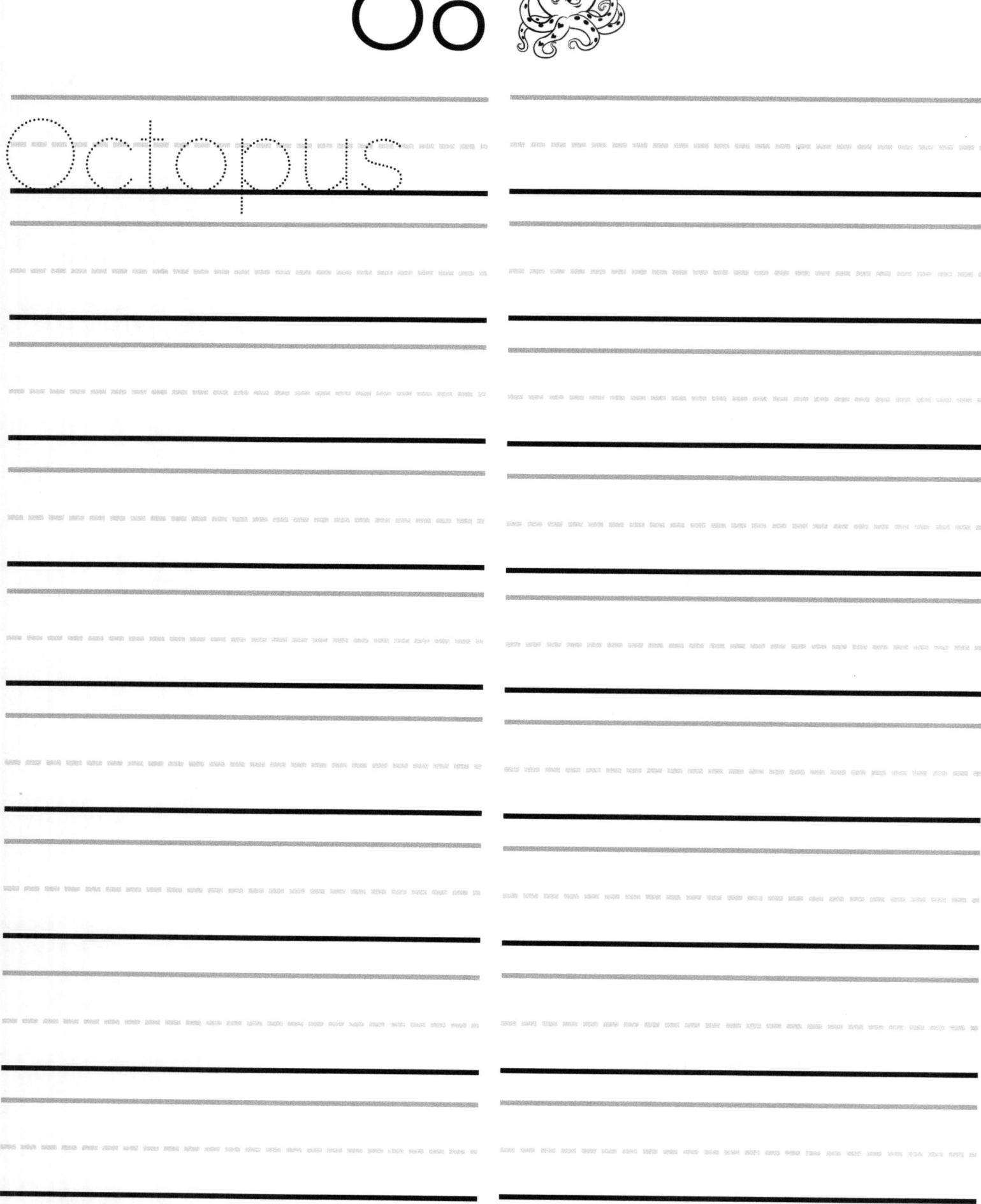

Octopus

You know what to do, Kiddywink Crew!
Draw your picture here!

SHIVERING PENGUINS

Directions: *July is the coldest month in Esperanza Base in Antarctica, where Penny the penguin lives. Create a* **line plot** *to show the temperatures in July one year.*

EXAMPLE:

August Temperatures in Esperanza Base					
12°F	14°F	10°F	14°F	13°F	13°F

19 degrees was already put on the line plot below. You may want to cross it out in the table! Fill in the rest of the numbers and x's on your line plot below.

July Temperatures in Esperanza Base					**19°F**
9°F	4°F	5°F	12°F	20°F	21°F
19°F	12°F	17°F	18°F	12°F	11°F
6°F	7°F	7°F	10°F	10°F	17°F
18°F	11°F	13°F	13°F	12°F	7°F
9°F	12°F	6°F	10°F	12°F	20°F

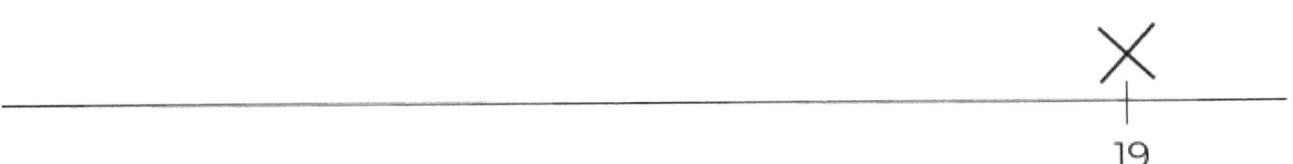

19

What was the warmest temperature in July? _____

What was the coldest temperature in July? _____

Which temperature happened the most in July? _____

KIDDYWINK

Pp

Penguin

Qq

You know what to do, Kiddywink Crew!
Draw your picture here!

Directions: Quinn the quail loves to watch baseball. His favorite player is the pitcher who wears a jersey with the number 17 on the back! He wanted all of the star jerseys below to **have 17 stars** on the back of each of them. Can you help him?

EXAMPLE:

12 + 5 = 17

_____ + _____ = 17

_____ + _____ = 17

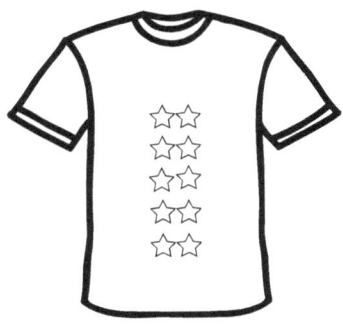

_____ + _____ = 17

_____ + _____ = 17

_____ + _____ = 17

_____ + _____ = 17

_____ + _____ = 17

_____ + _____ = 17

_____ + _____ = 17

KIDDYWINK CREW

Qq

Quail

R r

YOUR TURN!

You know what to do, Kiddywink Crew!
Draw your picture here!

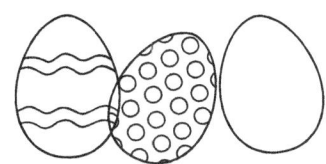 **REINDEERS HOLIDAY SMASHUP**

Directions: _The Reindeers were having a blast getting ready for their Holiday Smashup! Help them figure out how many different decorations they need. Feel free to draw out the decorations too if you want!_

Runar wanted to have 18 pumpkins for all the Halloween fun. He already had 10 pumpkins. How many more did he need?

Two of the reindeers wanted eggs for an Easter egg hunt. One of them found 12 eggs, and the other one found 4 eggs. How many did they have in all?

Ragnar wanted to make Christmas cookies. He bought two boxes of cookie mix. Each box makes 11 cookies. How many cookies can he make?

Another reindeer wanted to make Hanukkah latkes. She made 6 latkes in each batch. She made 3 batches. How many latkes did she make?

They also wanted fireworks to celebrate Diwali and New Year's. One reindeer went out and bought 50 fireworks! She had 5 packages and each package had the same amount of fireworks. How many did each package have?

Rr

Reindeer

YOUR TURN!

You know what to do, Kiddywink Crew!
Draw your picture here!

SANDY'S SILLY PARENTS LAUNCH MARSHMALLOWS

Directions: _Sandy's silly parents tried to wake her up with marshmallows! Help them figure out how many marshmallows they have left each day after_ **subtracting** _marshmallows from their pile and waking her up._

EXAMPLE:

On Monday they had 13 marshmallows. They threw 6 of them and then Sandy finally woke up! How many were left?

There were 7 marshmallows left!

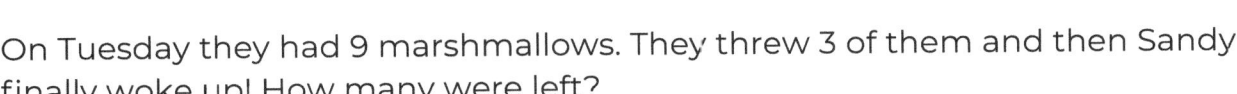

On Tuesday they had 9 marshmallows. They threw 3 of them and then Sandy finally woke up! How many were left?

On Wednesday they had 14 marshmallows. They threw 7 of them and then Sandy finally woke up! How many were left?

On Tuesday they had 11 marshmallows. They threw 5 of them and then Sandy finally woke up! How many were left?

On Tuesday they had 16 marshmallows. They threw 11 of them and then Sandy finally woke up! How many were left?

Ss

Sloth

Tt

YOUR TURN!

You know what to do, Kiddywink Crew!
Draw your picture here!

TESSA THE DECORATED TURTLE

Directions: _Timmy's friend, Tessa, always has pretty designs all over her shell. Today she wanted to have lots of colors on her body. Help her add color to the **shapes** on her shell!_

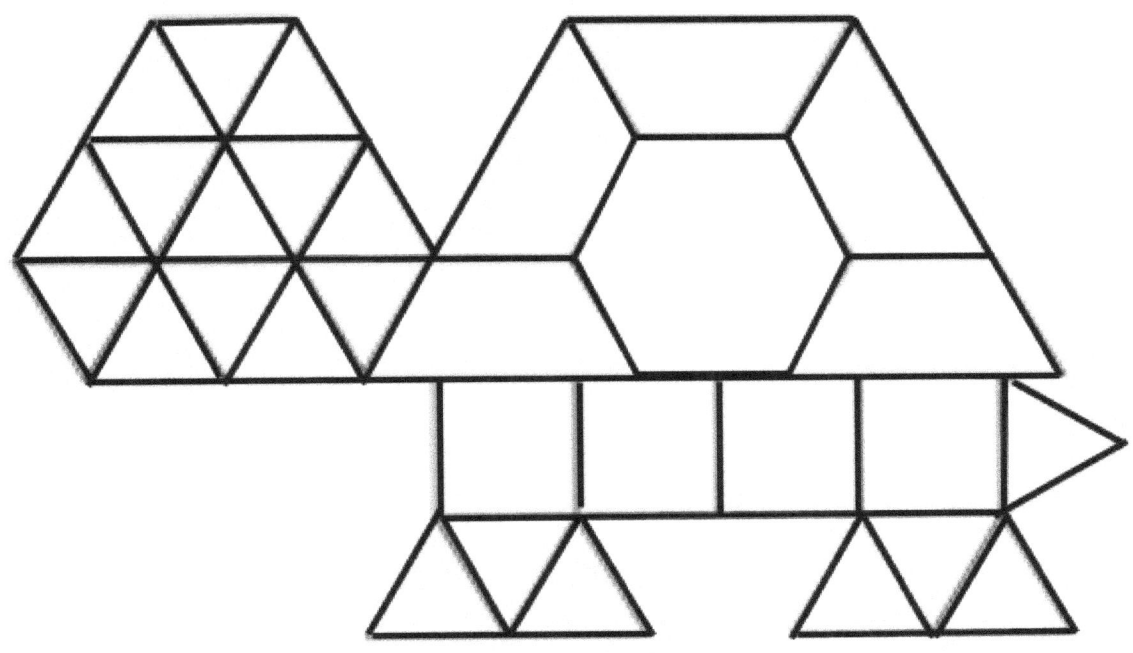

How many triangles are there? _____ triangles

What is half that amount? _____ triangles

Color half of the triangles green, and half of them yellow.

How many trapezoids are there? _____ trapezoids

Color the trapezoid(s) red. Color the hexagon(s) orange.

How many squares are there? _____ squares

What is half of that amount? _____ squares

Color half the squares blue and half of them purple.

Feel free to add any more decorations to her shell - she'd love whatever you do! And if you have pattern blocks at home you can try to recreate this image!

Tt

Turtle

Uu

You know what to do, Kiddywink Crew!
Draw your picture here!

UNEQUAL UMA

Directions: Uma the Umbrellabird loves inequalities. Help her solve the ones below before it rains on her! Use the symbols **> or < or =** in the raindrops to make each number sentence correct!

The greater number is on the side with two ends, and the lower number is on the side with one end.

 $10 > 2$

 $10 < 10 + 1$

EXAMPLE:

8 + 4 $>$ 12 - 1	7 - 2 ◯ 7 + 2
5 + 3 ◯ 4 + 4	13 + 2 ◯ 12 + 3
13 - 3 ◯ 2 + 3 + 3	9 + 7 ◯ 3 x 3
1 + 8 ◯ 14 - 3	3 + 6 ◯ 9 + 0 - 1
5 x 2 ◯ 20 - 10	12 - 7 ◯ 2 + 4
14 - 7 ◯ 1 + 5 + 2	6 + 7 ◯ 5 + 8
13 - 0 ◯ 8 + 7	10 + 2 ◯ 2 + 9 + 2

KIDDYWINK CREW

Uu

Umbrellabird

Vv

YOUR TURN!

You know what to do, Kiddywink Crew!
Draw your picture here!

90

Directions: Victoria runs any time she can, and she can make any road into a racetrack! Find something to use to **measure** these tracks. You can use a ruler, or you can find something unique, like paperclip(s) or goldfish cracker(s) or something else!

EXAMPLE:

Racetrack A is _6 PAPER CLIPS LONG_

Racetrack B is

Racetrack C is

Racetrack D is

Racetrack E is

Vv

Velociraptor

Ww

You know what to do, Kiddywink Crew!
Draw your picture here!

WALTER'S NECKLACES

Directions: *Walter loves to wear colorful necklaces. He especially likes when they have a pattern. Can you help him* **complete the pattern** *for each of his necklaces? Color them in too!*

P = PINK G = GREEN B = BLUE Y = YELLOW R = RED O = ORANGE

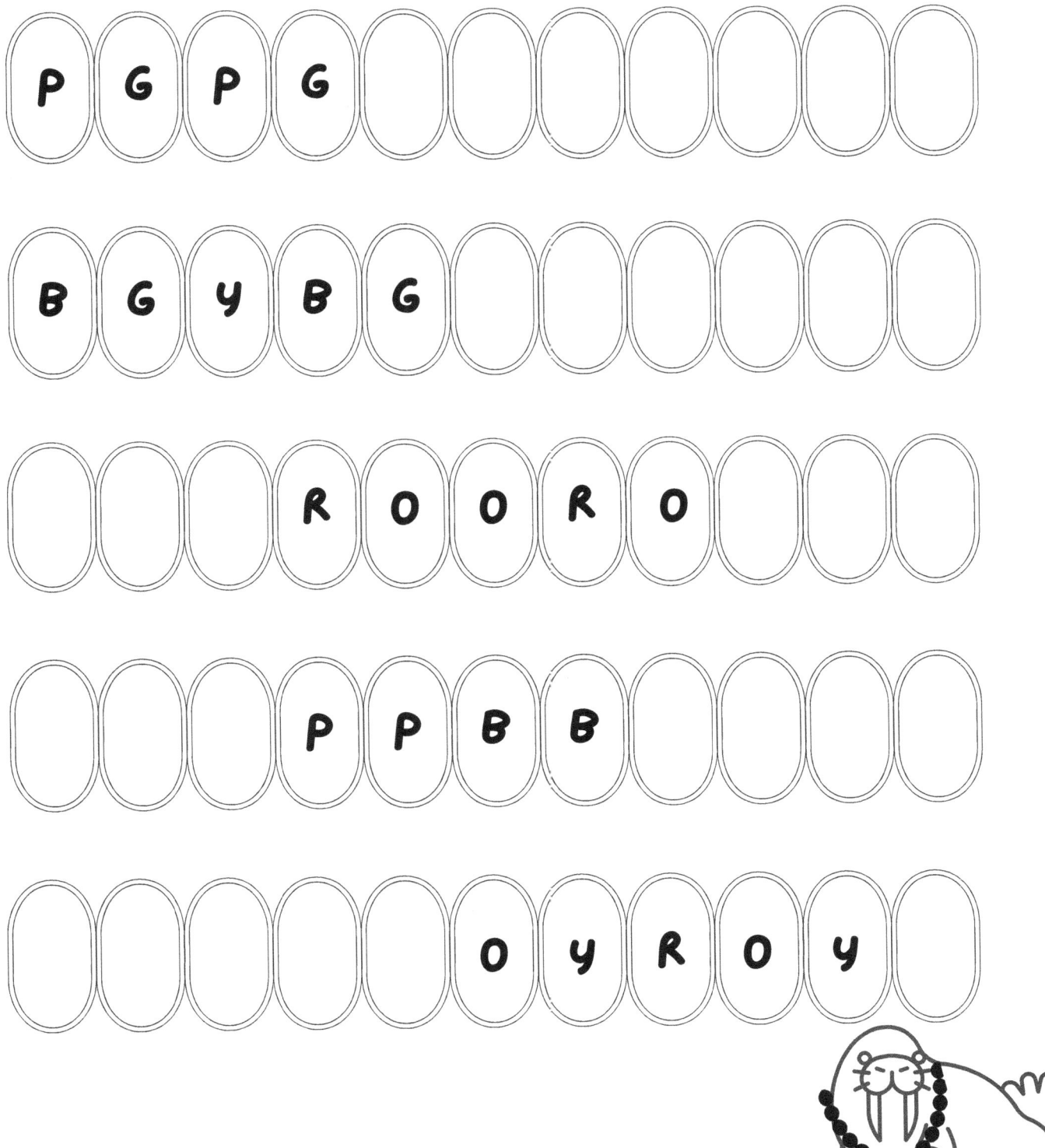

Row 1: P G P G

Row 2: B G Y B G

Row 3: R O O R O

Row 4: P P B B

Row 5: O Y R O Y

Ww

Walrus

Xx

YOUR TURN!

You know what to do, Kiddywink Crew!
Draw your picture here!

Directions: _Every time Xavier meets with Dr. Jen, some of his worries go away. Help him **subtract** worries and feel better!_

EXAMPLE:

Xavier went into his session with 10 worries. When he left he only had 4 worries. How many worries did he get rid of?

Equation: **10-6=4**

He got rid of 6 worries!

Xavier went into his session with _____ worries. When he left he only had 2 worries. How many worries did he get rid of?

Equation:

Xavier went into his session with _____ worries. When he left he only had 7 worries. How many worries did he get rid of?

Equation:

Xavier went into his session with _____ worries. When he left he only had 3 worries. How many worries did he get rid of?

Equation:

Xavier went into his session with _____ worries. When he left he only had 6 worries. How many worries did he get rid of?

Equation:

KIDDYWINK

Xx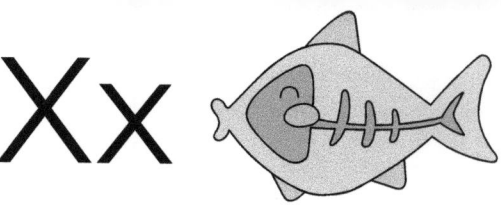

X-Ray Tetra

Yy

You know what to do, Kiddywink Crew!
Draw your picture here!

 YASMINE'S GARDEN

Directions: _Yasmine wanted to design a new garden for her class. She had a few different design ideas. Help her_ **complete each design plan** _with flowers, trees and carrots!_

Garden #1:

Divide into 4 equal sections. Put 3 flowers in each section. How many flowers are in this garden?

_____

Garden #2:

Divide into 3 equal sections. Plant 8 trees in each section. How many trees are in this garden?

_____

Garden #3:

Draw 3 rows of carrots with 9 carrots in each row. How many carrots are there in all?

_____

KIDDYWINK

Yy

Yak

You know what to do, Kiddywink Crew!
Draw your picture here!

ZESTY FOOD PUZZLES

Directions: *Zadie and Zora tried so many new foods! Can you solve these* **puzzles** *with some of the food they tried? Each picture represents a different whole number. The first puzzle is tricky and the second one is even trickier! Just try your best and have fun!*

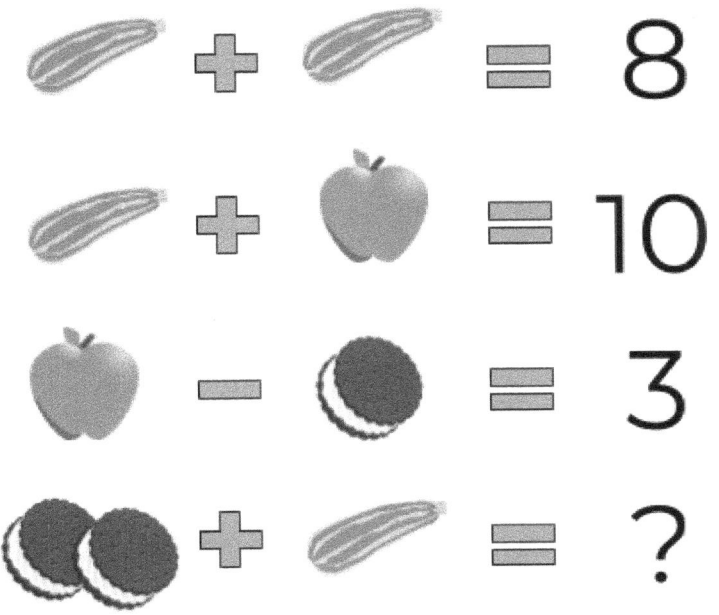

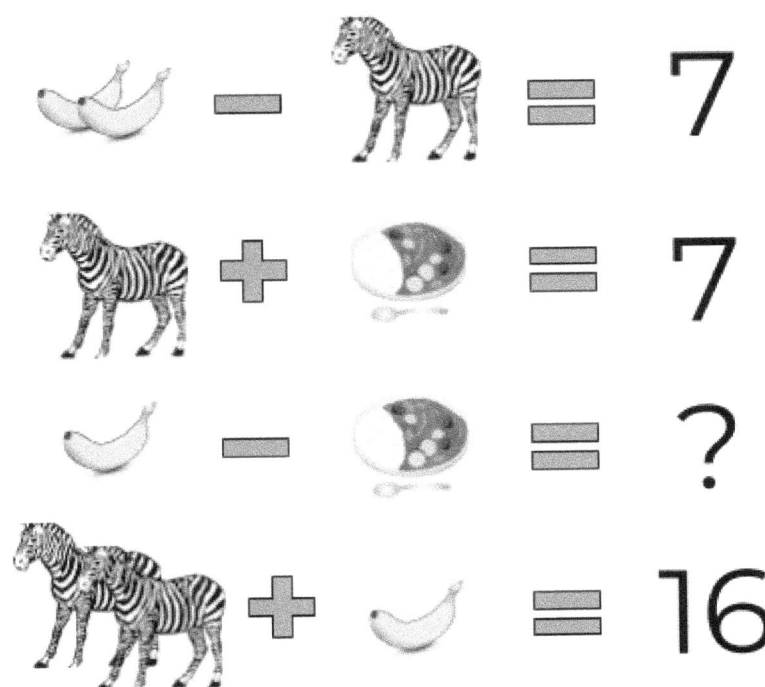

KIDDYWINK

Zz

Zebra

MATH STANDARDS
Checklist

Letter	PK	Counting & Cardinality		Operations & Algebraic Thinking				Numbers and Base Ten				Measurement & Data				Geometry			
	PK	K	1	K	1	2	3+	K	1	2	3+	K	1	2	3+	K	1	2	3+
A	✓	✓	✓	✓	✓														
B						✓													
C			✓		✓	✓	✓			✓									
D		✓	✓									✓	✓	✓	✓				
E					✓	✓			✓	✓			✓	✓	✓				
F	✓	✓	✓	✓	✓			✓	✓										
G		✓	✓	✓	✓	✓		✓	✓										
H														✓	✓				
I					✓	✓							✓	✓		✓	✓	✓	
J		✓	✓																
K					✓	✓													
L		✓	✓	✓	✓	✓													
M						✓	✓												
N					✓	✓	✓												
O						✓	✓												
P														✓	✓				
Q					✓	✓	✓												
R					✓	✓	✓												
S					✓	✓	✓												
T	✓	✓	✓	✓	✓	✓										✓	✓	✓	✓
U									✓	✓									
V	✓			✓								✓	✓	✓					
W	✓															✓			
X					✓	✓	✓												
Y	✓	✓	✓	✓	✓	✓	✓					✓				✓	✓	✓	✓
Z						✓	✓												

We are providing this table in hopes that it will be helpful. Please feel free to ignore it and let your child enjoy any and all of the math pages in whatever way they wish. This is mostly here to remind everyone that this activity book is for many ages, so some of the math work will be below or above your child's ability. Hopefully your child can return to pages that are too difficult at a later time. Most importantly, we hope all the pages are enjoyable, and make your days a little bit better!

Based on Illinois State Math Standards

KIDDYWINK CREW

THANKS YOU!!

TRULY, FROM THE BOTTOM OF OUR THREE HEARTS,
WE THANK YOU ALL FOR THE SUPPORT!
WE HOPE YOU ALL ENJOYED THIS ACTIVITY BOOK!

PLEASE CONSIDER LEAVING REVIEWS FOR OUR PODCAST, AND THIS BOOK.

Remember to listen
to the podcast!

SCAN THE
QR CODE

www.ingramcontent.com/pod-product-compliance
Lightning Source LLC
Chambersburg PA
CBHW041515120626

46551CB00018B/2446